D0425894

To Millie Schwanke

CAPRICORN

A guide to living your best astrological life

STELLA ANDROMEDA

ILLUSTRATED BY EVI O. STUDIO

Hardie Grant

BOOKS

Introduction   7

I.

Get to Know Capricorn

Capricorn characteristics   31
Physical Capricorn   34
How Capricorn communicates   37
Capricorn careers   38
How Capricorn chimes   41
Who loves whom?   44

II.

The Capricorn Deep Dive

The Capricorn home   55
Self-care   57
Food and cooking   59
How Capricorn handles money   61
How Capricorn handles the boss   62
What is Capricorn like to live with?   65
How to handle a break-up   66
How Capricorn wants to be loved   69
Capricorn's sex life   72

III.
Give Me More

Your birth chart   76
The Moon effect   80
The 10 planets   83
The four elements   89
Cardinal, fixed and mutable signs 92
The 12 houses   95
The ascendant   101
Saturn return   103
Mercury retrograde   104

Further reading   108
Acknowledgements   109
About the author   111

Introduction

Inscribed on the forecourt of the ancient Greek temple of Apollo at Delphi are the words 'know thyself'. This is one of the 147 Delphic maxims, or rules to live by, attributed to Apollo himself, and was later extended by the philosopher Socrates to the sentence, 'The unexamined life is not worth living.'

People seek a variety of ways of knowing themselves, of coming to terms with life and trying to find ways to understand the challenges of human existence, often through therapy or belief systems like organised religion. These are ways in which we strive to understand the relationships we have with ourselves and others better, seeking out particular tools that enable us to do so.

As far as systems of understanding human nature and experience go, astrology has much to offer through its symbolic use of the constellations of the heavens, the depictions of the zodiac signs, the planets and their energetic effects. Many people find accessing this information and harnessing its potential a useful way of thinking about how to manage their lives more effectively.

What is astrology?

In simple terms, astrology is the study and interpretation of how the planets can influence us, and the world in which we live, through an understanding of their positions at a specific place in time. The practice of astrology relies on a combination of factual knowledge of the characteristics of these positions and their psychological interpretation.

Astrology is less of a belief system and more of a tool for living, from which ancient and established wisdom can be drawn. Any of us can learn to use astrology, not so much for divination or telling the future, but as a guidebook that provides greater insight and a more thoughtful way of approaching life. Timing is very much at the heart of astrology, and knowledge of planetary configurations and their relationship to each other at specific moments in time can assist in helping us with the timing of some of our life choices and decisions.

Knowing when major life shifts can occur – because of particular planetary configurations such as a Saturn return (see page 103) or Mercury retrograde (see page 104) – or what it means to have Venus in your seventh house (see pages 85 and 98), while recognising the specific characteristics of your sign, are all tools that you can use to your advantage. Knowledge is power, and astrology can be a very powerful supplement to approaching life's ups and downs and any relationships we form along the way.

The 12 signs of the zodiac

Each sign of the zodiac has a range of recognisable characteristics, shared by people born under that sign. This is your Sun sign, which you probably already know – and the usual starting point from which we each begin to explore our own astrological paths. Sun sign characteristics can be strongly exhibited in an individual's make-up; however, this is only part of the picture.

Usually, how we appear to others is tempered by the influence of other factors – and these are worth bearing in mind. Your ascendant sign is equally important, as is the positioning of your Moon. You can also look to your opposite sign to see what your Sun sign may need a little more of, to balance its characteristics.

After getting to know your Sun sign in the first part of this book, you might want to dive into the Give Me More section (see pages 74–105) to start to explore all the particulars of your birth chart. These will give you far greater insight into the myriad astrological influences that may play out in your life.

Sun signs

It takes 365 (and a quarter, to be precise) days for the Earth to orbit the Sun and in so doing, the Sun appears to us to spend a month travelling through each sign of the zodiac. Your Sun sign is therefore an indication of the sign that the Sun was travelling through at the time of your birth. Knowing what Sun signs you and your family, friends and lovers are provides you with just the beginning of the insights into character and personality that astrology can help you discover.

On the cusp

For those for whom a birthday falls close to the end of one Sun sign and the beginning of another, it's worth knowing what time you were born. There's no such thing, astrologically, as being 'on the cusp' – because the signs begin at a specific time on a specific date, although this can vary a little year on year. If you are not sure, you'll need to know your birth date, birth time and birth place to work out accurately to which Sun sign you belong. Once you have these, you can consult an astrologer or run your details through an online astrology site program (see page 108) to give you the most accurate birth chart possible.

Taurus

The bull

21 APRIL-20 MAY

Aries

The ram

★

21 MARCH-20 APRIL

Astrologically the first sign of the zodiac, Aries appears alongside the vernal (or spring) equinox. A cardinal fire sign, depicted by the ram, it is the sign of beginnings and ruled by planet Mars, which represents a dynamic ability to meet challenges energetically and creatively. Its opposite sign is airy Libra.

Grounded, sensual and appreciative of bodily pleasures, Taurus is a fixed earth sign endowed by its ruling planet Venus with grace and a love of beauty, despite its depiction as a bull. Generally characterised by an easy and uncomplicated, if occasionally stubborn, approach to life, Taurus' opposite sign is watery Scorpio.

Gemini

The twins

✴

21 MAY–20 JUNE

A mutable air sign symbolised by the twins, Gemini tends to see both sides of an argument, its speedy intellect influenced by its ruling planet Mercury. Tending to fight shy of commitment, this sign also epitomises a certain youthfulness of attitude. Its opposite sign is fiery Sagittarius.

Cancer

The crab

✴

21 JUNE–21 JULY

Depicted by the crab and the tenacity of its claws, Cancer is a cardinal water sign, emotional and intuitive, its sensitivity protected by its shell. Ruled by the maternal Moon, the shell also represents the security of home, to which Cancer is committed. Its opposite sign is earthy Capricorn.

Leo

The lion

★

22 JULY–21 AUGUST

A fixed fire sign, ruled by the Sun, Leo loves to shine and is an idealist at heart, positive and generous to a fault. Depicted by the lion, Leo can roar with pride and be confident and uncompromising, with a great faith and trust in humanity. Its opposite sign is airy Aquarius.

Virgo

The virgin

★

22 AUGUST–21 SEPTEMBER

Traditionally represented as a maiden or virgin, this mutable earth sign is observant, detail oriented and tends towards self-sufficiency. Ruled by Mercury, Virgo benefits from a sharp intellect that can be self-critical, while often being very health conscious. Its opposite sign is watery Pisces.

Scorpio

The scorpion

✷

22 OCTOBER–21 NOVEMBER

Given to intense feelings, as
befits a fixed water sign, Scorpio
is depicted by the scorpion – linking
it to the rebirth that follows death –
and is ruled by both Pluto and Mars.
With a strong spirituality and deep
emotions, Scorpio needs security to
transform its strength. Its opposite
sign is earthy Taurus.

Libra

The scales

✷

22 SEPTEMBER–21 OCTOBER

A cardinal air sign, ruled by Venus,
Libra is all about beauty, balance
(as depicted by the scales) and
harmony in its rather romanticised,
ideal world. With a strong aesthetic
sense, Libra can be both arty and
crafty, but also likes fairness and
can be very diplomatic. Its
opposite sign is fiery Aries.

Sagittarius
The archer

★

22 NOVEMBER–21 DECEMBER

Depicted by the archer, Sagittarius is a mutable fire sign that's all about travel and adventure, in body or mind, and is very direct in approach. Ruled by the benevolent Jupiter, Sagittarius is optimistic with lots of ideas; liking a free rein, but with a tendency to generalise. Its opposite sign is airy Gemini.

Capricorn
The goat

★

22 DECEMBER–20 JANUARY

Ruled by Saturn, Capricorn is a cardinal earth sign associated with hard work and depicted by the sure-footed and sometimes playful goat. Trustworthy and unafraid of commitment, Capricorn is often very self-sufficient and has the discipline for the freelance working life. Its opposite sign is the watery Cancer.

Pisces

The fish

*

20 FEBRUARY–20 MARCH

Acutely responsive to its surroundings, Pisces is a mutable water sign depicted by two fish, swimming in opposite directions, sometimes confusing fantasy with reality. Ruled by Neptune, its world is fluid, imaginative and empathetic, often picking up on the moods of others. Its opposite sign is earthy Virgo.

Aquarius

The water carrier

*

21 JANUARY–19 FEBRUARY

Confusingly, given its depiction by the water carrier, Aquarius is a fixed air sign ruled by the unpredictable Uranus, sweeping away old ideas with innovative thinking. Tolerant, open-minded and all about humanity, its vision is social with a conscience. Its opposite sign is fiery Leo.

Get to

I.

Know

Capricorn

The sign the Sun
was travelling in at the
time you were born is the
ultimate starting point
in exploring your character
and personality through
the zodiac.

YOUR SUN SIGN

Cardinal earth sign, depicted
by the goat (with a fishy tail).

Ruled by Saturn, a Roman god
responsible for the sowing and
reaping of seeds, representing graft
and the patient wait for a return.

OPPOSITE SIGN

Cancer

STATEMENT OF SELF

'I use.'

Lucky colour

Earthy tones of brown and dark green are Capricorn's lucky colours, whose ideals are firmly rooted in the here and now. Wear these colours particularly when you need a psychological boost and additional courage. If you don't want to fully commit head-to-toe, choose darker or lighter tones for accessories – shoes, gloves, socks, hat or even underwear.

Lucky day

Saturday, Saturn's day and considered the seventh day of the week, and also the Sabbath day according to the book of Exodus in the Old Testament of the Bible, a day of rest for conscientious and hard-working Capricorns.

Lucky gem

The garnet is associated with abundance, self-empowerment and prosperity, and is also thought to link to the powerful, revitalising energies of the Earth. It represents willpower, too, and a strength of purpose that helps overcome difficulties – both very Capricorn abilities.

Locations

The industrious and hard-working nations of India, Bulgaria, the UK, Afghanistan, Haiti and the Sudan all resonate with Capricorn qualities. Cities that link to this sign include Oxford, Brandenburg, Delhi, Brussels, Chicago and Mexico City.

Holidays

It can be tricky for such a hard-working soul as
Capricorn to take a holiday, but they do like to be around
family or friends to replenish their batteries. They may also
choose to volunteer with a conservation project to protect
endangered species, or sports coaching with disadvantaged
kids. Alternatively, mountain trekking on foot or
rock climbing may appeal!

Flowers

The carnation with its long life, and pansies that reflect
Capricorn's thoughtful nature, are both Capricorn flowers;
along with ivy, known for its strong climbing!

VII.

Trees

There's a strength and durability about the tall pines that grow up mountainsides, weathering all seasons, that reflect Capricorn's qualities. The elm, too, is straight and enduring, like Capricorn.

VIII.

Pets

A ferret can make a delightful pet for Capricorn.
Naturally quiet but inquisitive, they make intelligent and
companionable pets, and need the sort of good, loving care
that Capricorn can provide.

Parties

When it comes to partying, Capricorn prefers formal events:
a lavish dinner where they can dress up in style, or a ball
with a small orchestra and dancing. They're social souls,
and events like New Year's Eve or a wedding call for
well-organised parties – a task at which Capricorn can
excel. When it comes to drinks, the earthiness of
a Grand Marnier on the rocks always appeals.

Capricorn characteristics

Sometimes considered rather a boring sign, it would be a mistake to dismiss Capricorn in this way. Cool, creative, ambitious, diligent and with a wry sense of humour, dig a little deeper and they are anything but. Capricorn is an interesting combination of being a practical earth sign linked to strong initiative by courtesy of being a cardinal sign. Ruled by Saturn, the large celestial taskmaster of the skies, Capricorn is a real grafter with BIG dreams, which they are ambitious enough to follow. It can take 10 years to become an overnight success, which sounds like a contradiction in terms, but that's Capricorn, grafting away until they hit the big time in whichever field they choose. They achieve great heights, like a sure-footed mountain goat, but it always comes from diligent and creative hard work.

There is a reserve to Capricorn that's often mistaken for aloofness and it's true that they take time to consider the facts, basing decisions on these rather than gut instinct. This realism is a very attractive trait because it also means that life's ups and downs don't scare Capricorn – they've got it covered and know they can handle it, which instils confidence in others. This realism can sometimes be seen as stubbornness but that's not true, it's just that Capricorn needs to be sure of things and they take their time to get it right. And, above all, the person they depend on most to get it right is themselves.

All this taking their time can make Capricorn seem a bit elusive because decision-making is something that won't be rushed. There's also a deeply private streak that comes from a strong self-reliance, which can make them appear a bit of a loner, but they love to love and be loved as much as anyone. And anyone who cherishes a Capricorn will be well rewarded, as they make true and reliable friends and lovers – kind and supportive once they're committed – and their devotion shouldn't be underrated.

What is also true about Capricorn, and often unexpected, is their very good sense of humour. Neither pompous nor stuffy, Capricorn has a shrewd and ironic take on life that can be both refreshing and very amusing. Like other earth signs, Capricorn is capable of taking great sensual pleasure in life, and they relax in the right mood and with people who matter to them. Once Capricorn has loosened up, and they have to feel secure enough to do so, they're as much fun as anyone.

LOOSENING
THE EARTH

The key characteristics of any
Sun sign can be balanced out
(or sometimes reinforced) by the
characteristics of other signs in the
same birth chart, particularly those
of the ascendant and the Moon. So
if someone doesn't appear to be
typical of their Sun sign, that's why.
However, those nascent Capricorn
aspects will always be there as
a key influence, informing an
individual's approach to life.

Physical
Capricorn

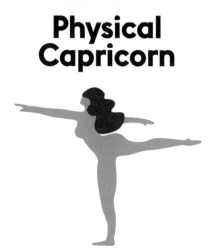

Physically confident and well-coordinated, Capricorn's body movements tend to be deft and purposeful, sure-footed and with little wasted effort. Their physique tends to look lithe and well-balanced, their gaze direct, sure of their path. It's as if they have a clear image of where they're going and how they're going to get there, which is generally true. There's an energy about them that feels very secure and a purposeful stillness when they are stationary that conveys reassurance. And because there is something very grounded but alert about their physical appearance, Capricorn makes other people feel safe just by being there.

Health

Capricorn has a physical strength that makes them hardy by nature and pretty resilient generally. When they do fall ill, Capricorn tends to recover quickly, partly because they are sensible enough to allow themselves enough time to recover. You won't find them soldiering on with a high temperature, they're much too socially minded for that and like to keep their bugs at home to avoid infecting everyone else. One area of weakness for Capricorn tends to be their bones and joints (knees in particular), making the occasional accidental bruise, sprain or fracture a problem, while arthritis and other orthopaedic problems may also be troublesome in later life.

Exercise

Exercise comes easily to Capricorn, who can be found bounding up the stairs rather than taking the lift. They will usually take any opportunity to factor activity into their daily life – walking to work or the shops when they can – in order to protect their overall health. The gym or communal exercise classes or team sports also appeal to socially minded Capricorn, but they're not particularly competitive in this arena, so one-to-one sports like tennis are less likely to feature.

How Capricorn communicates

It's not difficult to engage the full attention of Capricorn because they are always interested in the facts and evaluating the situation, so they know it helps to listen. But they do listen better if the issue is addressed directly without any beating about the bush, so time-wasters may get short shrift. That said, Capricorn's natural inclination is to listen and consider carefully, particularly about things that matter to them, whether this is personal politics or work agendas, and they usually choose their words with care.

Capricorn isn't a fan of small talk (and this can extend to flirting, too) but can debate with the best of them as long as it's something relevant or about which they have a genuine interest. However, they seldom waste words arguing for argument's sake. If Capricorn is really interested, you get full-beam attention and if they like you, they'll demonstrate this through what they do. Life's too short to play games in Capricorn's book.

Capricorn careers

Organisation comes easily to most Capricorns and they understand the nature of organisations, which can be a big plus in today's world. Combined with their grounded, sociable natures, working in big companies is something they relate to. What's also true is that within any organisation, Capricorn is very likely to find themselves working towards the top, whether they mean to or not. It just comes naturally to them to see the bigger picture, then work out how to achieve it. Within a company, Capricorns can be found as chief executives, human resource managers, financial planners or business analysts. The task is to find jobs like these in industries or organisations that appeal, which could be in banking, advertising, film or even teaching.

The law can be a good career for Capricorn, with its necessity for detailed consideration. Building in one form or another, from actually building a house to designing one as an architect or interior designer, also has its attractions, as does designing theatre or movie sets, particularly if optimising a budget is part of the process.

How Capricorn chimes

From lovers to friends, when it comes to other signs, how does Capricorn get along? Knowledge of other signs and how they interact can be helpful when negotiating relationships, revealed through an understanding of Sun sign characteristics that might chime or chafe. Understanding these through an astrological framework can be really helpful as it can depersonalise potential frictions, taking the sting out of what appears to be in opposition.

Harmonising relationships can sometimes appear to be a problem to ponder, rather than an opportunity to explore, to Capricorn. However, how they chime is partly dependent on what other planetary influences are at play in their personal birth chart, toning down or enhancing aspects of their Sun sign characteristics, especially those that can sometimes clash with other signs.

The Capricorn woman

There's a deftness and capability about the Capricorn woman that says, 'I'm for real, I know where I'm going and how I'm going to get there.' This could be a little daunting for the faint hearted! Very private, yes, but with a strong romantic streak, she's discriminating in her choice of partner and would rather not date at all than waste her time on the wrong person.

NOTABLE CAPRICORN WOMEN

Michelle Obama sums up the Capricorn woman: strongly feminine, determined and definite, with a flair for fun. As does Catherine, Duchess of Cambridge, who played a long game and patiently stuck it out for her prince. Singer Dolly Parton, model Kate Moss and that doyenne of British actresses, Dame Maggie Smith, are all extremely feminine Capricorns with an inner strength.

The Capricorn man

There's a lot hidden behind the frank, often earthy approach of this attractive loner. For a Capricorn on a career ladder, there may not be time for a great romance, even though this is what his heart may crave. It takes a smart partner to see beyond Capricorn's cool exterior to his more poetic side, which will only emerge when he feels secure in his affections.

NOTABLE CAPRICORN MEN

Enigmatic, ambitious David Bowie was a grafter who remained true to his dreams, while Lin-Manuel Miranda's award-winning musical *Hamilton* was an 'overnight success' after years of work. Actors Bradley Cooper and Eddie Redmayne show similar Capricorn traits, making interesting choices to climb to the top of their careers.

Who love

Capricorn & Aries

Aries' impulsive nature is an immediate problem for many Capricorns, who need to take time over decisions and may find it difficult to believe that a commitment from this outgoing fire sign is even possible. Often great friends, though, as both share ambition.

Capricorn & Taurus

Two sensual earthy signs with a lot in common, both value their security and relish creating a home. Both also admire each other's strengths, while Taurus' affectionate stability helps overcome Capricorn's caution, allowing passion and romance to flourish.

Capricorn & Gemini

Once the initial attraction has passed, there can be a problem. Gemini's excitable extravagance will try Capricorn's conservative patience on just about every front, while their airy verbal wit can make this earth sign feel a tad stodgy and inadequate.

Capricorn & Cancer

Zodiac opposites, there are complementary features, but also a chasm between Cancer's need for security and constant reassurance, and Capricorn's, which is more to do with bricks and mortar. There's a strong sexual attraction, but after that, all bets are off!

Capricorn & Leo

Even if there's an initial attraction, Capricorn can't really understand Leo's exuberance and egotistical ways, finding these difficult to tolerate. The daily dose of adoration Leo needs is a demand too far for reserved, discriminating Capricorn.

Capricorn & Virgo

Each is appreciative of the other's neat and organised approach, their intellectual style and capacity for working hard, making this a harmonious coupling. The only downside might be that with so much reticence on both sides, the relationship could stagnate.

Capricorn & Scorpio

This is a surprisingly good match given they're both so strong willed, but Capricorn's need for security is well met by Scorpio's possessiveness, which provides a powerful bond. And if their tempers clash and the sparks fly, it also fuels their romance.

Capricorn & Libra

Libra's artistic appreciation, love of luxury and work/life balance can initially attract Capricorn, but over time there's a clash about responsibility and discipline and the earth sign's jealousy doesn't help either.

Capricorn & Sagittarius

Sagittarius' optimism is wonderfully invigorating to Capricorn's reserve, encouraging a lighter view of life, but in time this could begin to feel undermining, as if they're not being taken seriously – a problem that Sagittarius can't really fathom.

Capricorn &
Aquarius

Aquarius' unpredictable style
unnerves Capricorn, who prefers
organisation and schedules, and
this irritates Aquarius. However,
underneath all this is an appreciation
of their very different qualities, which
can make them friends if not lovers.

Capricorn &
Pisces

A lovely union can exist because
Capricorn finds Pisces' imagination
enhances their dreams, while
their ability to graft fuels a mutual
commitment. Pisces' affectionate
nature makes Capricorn feel secure,
and this works well in the bedroom, too.

Capricorn &
Capricorn

Compatible on almost all
fronts, from attitudes to work,
approach to socialising and
even to money, there's full-on
mutual appreciation that bodes
well in the bedroom, too. But
the possible flaw to all this is
that there's a tendency for life
to be a bit ... dull.

Capricorn love-o-meter

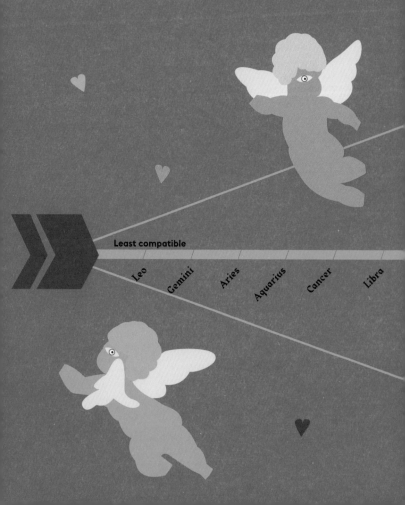

Least compatible

Leo   Gemini   Aries   Aquarius   Cancer   Libra

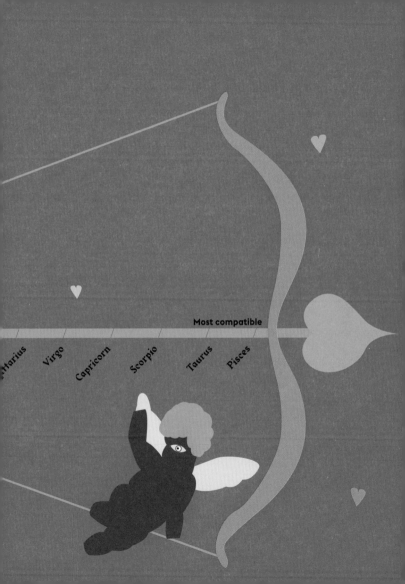

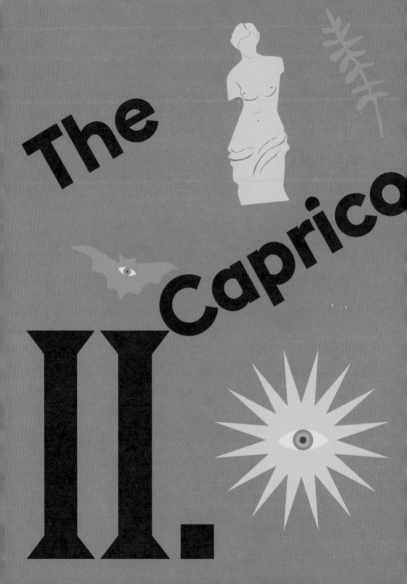

Deep Dive

In this section, dive deeper into the ways in which your Sun sign might be driving you or holding you back, and start to think about how you might use this knowledge to inform your path.

The
Capricorn
home

When it comes to their home, Capricorn likes furnishings that stand the test of time and this might include some family heirlooms amongst state-of-the-art, beautifully constructed modern items. They also like a home to show off what they've attained in life and are prepared to spend lavishly on items that reflect this. Sometimes, though, the Capricorn instinct for iconic pieces can be more stylish than comfortable and there will need to be a compromise. So that modernist Wassily chair may be more for show than sitting on, and Capricorn will be utilising plush cushions to ensure a degree of comfort.

Mostly, though, Capricorn is realistic enough to know that a home is to live in, and however high a value they place on craftsmanship, they want somewhere that makes them feel secure and where they can relax after working hard. It will be well organised though, because too much clutter is unsettling, and they like it to be tidy, even if they don't favour a minimalist style. There's probably a nicely co-ordinated feel, too, with lots of earthy Capricorn colours, and they're likely to be familiar with both interior designers and high-end paint suppliers.

TOP TIPS FOR CAPRICORN SELF-CARE

* Take a regular look at work/life balance and be (even) more realistic.

* Don't miss out on enjoying life when heading for the top.

* Factor in some exercises to keep leg muscles strong.

Self-care

One of the most self-reliant Sun signs, Capricorn generally has very little difficulty looking after themselves, and the rest of their tribe while they're at it, but are not so good at being looked after, should they ever need it. While this is all well and good, it means that they can also be their own worst enemy and stoical to a fault, which can be infuriating for those who care about them. What's more, this extreme willpower means that they can sometimes push themselves too hard and too far, and then have to take time out to recover – which they hate. Turns out, the zodiac's worse patient may well be a Capricorn!

For a sign that keeps themselves and their thoughts very much to themselves, this can sometimes lead to introspection of an unhelpful kind. Combined with pushing themselves, some Capricorns can find their energy drained and their bodies and minds rebelling, which might find them self-medicating with alcohol rather than taking time off or asking for help to recover. Generally, though, Capricorn is too sensible to let this happen and if they are not naturally good at pacing themselves, they learn to do so, partly because they know they can achieve more if they stay on top of their game rather than fall over from exhaustion.

WHAT TO KEEP IN THE CAPRICORN PANTRY

* A jar of homemade roasted garlic in olive oil to add depth to any dish.

* Bouillon cubes for those days when chicken stock is just too much trouble.

* Nutty-flavoured super-grain amaranth – high in protein and can be 'popped' like popcorn for a fast snack.

Food
and
cooking

Food is essentially fuel for Capricorn, something that ensures they can continue their industrious life. They enjoy eating, especially when sharing a meal with family or friends, but cooking isn't a huge priority. Their kitchens may be highly organised with lots of helpful gadgets, but it's not where Capricorn creativity is best expressed, not least because they would prefer food to behave in a predictable, orderly fashion without allowing for its possible alchemy. When a recipe doesn't go to plan, they're likely to throw it out and order takeaway rather than try again.

Cooking works best for Capricorn when there's plenty of time and it can all be organised in advance. Formal events live up to this rather better than spontaneous meals or kitchen suppers. Capricorn is less able to rustle up a delicious risotto from leftovers than a meticulously prepared beef Wellington. Add a dose of competitiveness, and it's then that Capricorn might sparkle in the kitchen.

TOP TIPS FOR CAPRICORN'S MONEY

★ Don't be too conservative about investments, a little risk is okay.

★ Plan for retirement, yes; but also enjoy some of life's pleasures along the way.

★ Remember, the occasional impulse buy won't break the bank.

How Capricorn handles money

With a basic concern for security, Capricorn often looks for a strong financial underpinning to their life, for which they're prepared to work hard. And as a consequence of this, they are likely to be conservative, if not cautious, about money. There's no doubt that all Capricorn's carefulness pays off and they tend to have healthy bank accounts, even becoming wealthy in time. That old saying, 'Look after the pennies and the pounds will look after themselves,' must surely have first been said by a Capricorn. They tend to be risk averse and any investments are likely to be well researched and evaluated before purchase. Capricorn understands better than anyone the value of money, that it represents accomplishment and that it is a commodity that can be used to good effect. They know how to work it to make it work for them, too. Sure, they can be thrifty, but once committed to a financial course of action, it's likely to pay off.

How Capricorn handles the boss

Reliable to a fault, Capricorn turns up on time, anticipates their boss' needs and gets the job done with minimum fuss. All well and good, but Capricorn's commitment to their own job may be a means to an end and what they're working towards is actually their boss' job ... which needs to be handled carefully. Although Capricorn's renowned capability is seldom matched by others, in handling their boss it's as well to stay aware of the limitations – as well as the possibilities – of their own work role, in order to keep the boss sweet.

Career advancement can happen fast for hard-working Capricorns, once they've discovered their happiest working environment, and that's probably inside a company where they feel secure, and often a large one at that. But another Capricorn trait is the capacity to put the good of the whole before their own personal aims, in order to ensure the whole team functions well. Capricorn might not like to waste time in meetings, but meeting and communicating well with their superiors is a good ploy for keeping them on side. That done, Capricorn can forge their own path through any potential office politics, to ensure they stay on course for their own success.

TOP TIPS TO HANDLE THE BOSS

* Be patient in meetings; not everyone gets to the point as quickly as Capricorn.

* In working your way up, make an ally of the boss by being accommodating.

* Remind your boss that you sometimes take your time, but the results speak for themselves.

TOP TIPS FOR
AN EASIER LIFE

★ Try not to mind if things aren't done *exactly* as you'd like them.

★ Go with the flow occasionally; spontaneity is important.

★ Factor in some fun times – life is for living not just work.

What is Capricorn like to live with?

As long as housemates or partners are similarly inclined – that is, generally quite reserved, well organised and tidy – then living with Capricorn is pretty simple. Clashes can occur, however, when Capricorn comes home after another long day to discover that the dishwasher hasn't been stacked properly or that the laundry pile is tottering in the corner. It seems so simple to Capricorn to stay on top of things that they can never fathom why anyone would do it differently. And if communal living is involved, you can bet there's a chores rota tacked to the kitchen wall. In some cases, they may well feel obliged to organise the whole household – not just the chores but also social events.

As long as they're not working on a deadline and the washing up's been done, Capricorn can be relatively relaxed company. They're genuinely social and like having people around, and don't often feel the need to disappear off on their own to recharge their batteries. Planning is key, as they are generous hosts and prefer to make sure everything is just right for their guests, rather than take pot luck, so anyone attempting a spontaneous visit may raise a quizzical Capricorn eyebrow.

How to
handle a
break-up

A pragmatist with a strongly practical streak, Capricorn can often appear rather a cool customer if their relationship breaks up. Whether or not they've instigated it, they tend to take a practical approach: it wasn't working, so best to move on and – this is very Capricorn – least said, soonest mended. No hard feelings. The trouble is, having made a deep commitment in order to have a relationship in the first place, it probably cuts deeper than it appears to resilient Capricorn. Their ex might think from their behaviour that there's no residual feelings to honour, but it won't be true. Having loved and lost (for whatever reason), Capricorn finds it takes time to recover. Not for them the rebound romance, and this is how an ex will know how much they once mattered.

TOP TIPS FOR AN EASIER BREAK-UP

* Forget the stiff upper lip, a break-up is sad and it's okay to express this.

* Remember it's acceptable just to date and have some fun occasionally.

* Don't dismiss a future partner because they don't immediately tick all the right boxes.

How Capricorn wants to be loved

Feeling secure is an important part of how Capricorn wants to be loved. It's not that they are needy types, far from it, but Capricorn's emotional self-reliance is also something of a defence against time wasting, which only feeling secure can overcome. It takes a smart suitor to see that any emotional reserve can be part of their sizing up process, and only when they are 100 per cent sure of whoever's courting them will that person be rewarded with a show of interest.

Contrary to outward appearance, Capricorn is also a sign that likes to be pursued and wooed. Idealistic, yes, but this also includes being idealistic about romance of the obvious kind – red roses, anyone? – only it has to be authentic. Capricorn is very canny about other people's motivations, and it may feel a bit as if someone has to prove themselves time and time again. Capricorn wants to be loved completely but are realistic enough to know how hard it is to find a true soul mate. This links to the value they place on relationships, which in their book are crucial, but there's little inclination to waste time on something that may be of no value. If this sounds harsh, it's because love is so important to Capricorn that they may well be prepared to forgo it for anything less than the real thing.

While romance is definitely important, it is also unlikely to be prioritised by Capricorn over future considerations. Is this person the 'one' for the future? Capricorn always looks to the future and plans for it, so they want to be loved by someone who has a similar view of a shared future. Given their private natures, it's only by paying close attention that it will be possible to work out how Capricorn wants to be loved.

There's a balance to be struck, however, because Capricorn is also – like other earth signs – sensual and very much aware of physical pleasure, which they relish. They recognise that it's often a way in which it's possible to get to know someone else, and they can be quite realistic about this, too. Physical love is a direct expression of mental love for many Capricorns, and this earthy side can sometimes surprise, given their tendency towards caution. You can bet your bottom dollar, however, that any move is only ever made after carefully judging a situation. And once they commit, it's total and unlikely to wane.

TOP TIPS FOR
LOVING CAPRICORN

★ Take your time: loving
  Capricorn is a marathon
  not a sprint.

★ Capricorn tends to be very
  independent, but they need
  to feel secure to feel loved.

★ If you can't talk about it
  (whatever it is), it's hard
  to woo them.

Capricorn's sex life

Capricorns tend to be earthy sensualists with a strong sex drive. They are generally happy in their bodies and like to express love with an almost poetic physicality. Not for them a hasty experience in a hay field, they want to take their time in comfort and warmth and soft lighting. It's not luxury so much that Capricorn is after, but to feel secure enough to express themselves and this may take a certain amount of forethought and planning. It may sound contradictory but, for Capricorn, being spontaneous in bed takes thought and time.

Sexual fidelity is often the rule with Capricorn; once committed they're loyal and can be quite conservative on this front. And although a Capricorn likes to be talked into bed – mental stimulation is important – once they've decided to get down to it, they won't want to waste time talking further. That said, once comfortable and secure they're not afraid to say what they like and what they want from their lover. And Capricorn looks for a recognisably equal lover who is as accomplished and self-confident as they are themselves. All this may sound rather exacting, which is a Capricorn trait, but once securely attached all this loosens up in a beautiful way.

Me More

Your Sun sign never shows you the whole picture. In this section, learn how to read the nuances of your birth chart and discover a whole new level of astrological insight.

Your birth chart

Your birth chart is a snapshot of a particular moment, in a particular place, at the precise moment of your birth and is therefore completely individual to you. It's like a blueprint, a map, a statement of occurrence, spelling out possible traits and influences – but it isn't your destiny. It is just a symbolic tool to which you can refer, based on the position of the planets at the time of your birth. If you can't get to an astrologer, these days anyone can get their birth chart prepared in minutes online (see page 108 for a list of websites and apps that will do it for you). Even if you don't know your exact time of birth, just knowing the date and place of birth can create the beginnings of a useful template.

Remember, nothing is intrinsically good or bad in astrology and there is no explicit timing or forecasting: it's more a question of influences and how these might play out positively or negatively. And if we have some insight, and some tools with which to approach, see or interpret our circumstances and surroundings, this gives us something to work with.

When you are reading your birth chart, it's useful to first understand all the tools of astrology available to you; not only the astrological signs and what they represent, but also the 10 planets referred to in astrology and their individual characteristics, along with the 12 houses and what they mean. Individually, these tools of astrology are of passing interest, but when you start to see how they might sit in juxtaposition to each other, then the bigger picture becomes more accessible and we begin to gain insights that can be useful to us.

Broadly speaking, each of the planets suggests a different type of energy, the astrological signs propose the various ways in which that energy might be expressed, while the houses represent areas of experience in which this expression might operate.

Next to bring into the picture are the positions of the signs at four key points: the ascendant, or rising sign, and its opposite, the descendant; and the midheaven and its opposite, the IC, not to mention the different aspects created by congregations of signs and planets.

It is now possible to see how subtle the reading of a birth chart might be and how it is infinite in its variety, and highly specific to an individual. With this information, and a working understanding of the symbolic meaning and influences of the signs, planets and houses of your unique astrological profile, you can begin to use these tools to help with decision-making and other aspects of life.

Reading your chart

If you have your birth chart prepared, either by hand or via an online program, you will see a circle divided into 12 segments, with information clustered at various points indicating the position of each zodiac sign, in which segment it appears and at what degree. Irrespective of the features that are relevant to the individual, each chart follows the same pattern when it comes to interpretation.

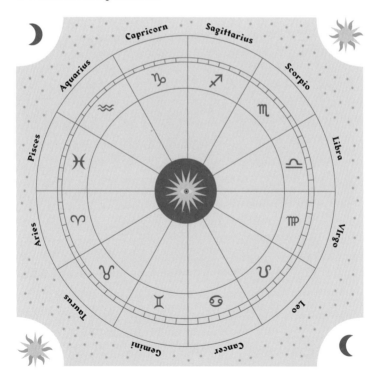

Given the time of birth, the place of birth and the position of the planets at that moment, the birth chart, sometimes called a natal horoscope, is drawn up.

If you consider the chart as a clock face, the first house (see pages 95–99 for the astrological houses) begins at the 9, and it is from this point that, travelling anti-clockwise the chart is read from the first house, through the 12 segments of the chart to the twelfth.

The beginning point, the 9, is also the point at which the Sun rises on your life, giving you your ascendant, or rising sign, and opposite to this, at the 3 of the clock face, is your descendant sign. The midheaven point of your chart, the MC, is at 12, and its opposite, the IC, at 6 (see pages 101–102).

Understanding the significance of the characteristics of the astrological signs and the planets, their particular energies, their placements and their aspects to each other can be helpful in understanding ourselves and our relationships with others. In day-to-day life, too, the changing configuration of planets and their effects are much more easily understood with a basic knowledge of astrology, as are the recurring patterns that can sometimes strengthen and sometimes delay opportunities and possibilities. Working with, rather than against, these trends can make life more manageable and, in the last resort, more successful.

The Moon effect

If your Sun sign represents your consciousness, your life force and your individual will, then the Moon represents that side of your personality that you tend to keep rather secret or hidden. This is the realm of instinct, intuition, creativity and the unconscious, which can take you places emotionally that are sometimes hard to understand. This is what brings great subtlety and nuance to a person, way beyond just their Sun sign. So you may have your Sun in Capricorn, and all that means, but this might be countered by a strongly empathetic and feeling Moon in Cancer; or you may have your Sun in open-hearted Leo, but a Moon in Aquarius with all its rebellious, emotional detachment.

Phases of the Moon

The Moon orbits the Earth, taking roughly 28 days to do so. How much of the Moon we see is determined by how much of the Sun's light it reflects, giving us the impression that it waxes, or grows, and wanes. When the Moon is new, to us, only a sliver of it is illuminated. As it waxes, it reflects more light and moves from a crescent, to a waxing crescent to a first quarter; then it moves to a waxing gibbous Moon, to a full Moon. Then the Moon begins to wane through a waning gibbous, to a last quarter, and then the cycle begins again. All of this occurs over four weeks. When we have two full Moons in any one calendar month, the second is called a blue Moon.

Each month the Moon also moves through an astrological sign, as we know from our personal birth charts. This, too, will yield information – a Moon in Scorpio can have a very different effect to one in Capricorn – and depending on our personal charts, this can have a shifting influence each month. For example, if the Moon in your birth chart is in Virgo, then when the actual Moon moves into Virgo, this will have an additional influence. Read the characteristics of the signs for further information (see pages 12–17).

The Moon's cycle has an energetic effect, which we can see quite easily on the ocean tides. Astrologically, because the Moon is both a fertility symbol and attuned to our deeper psychological side, we can use this to focus more profoundly and creatively on aspects of life that are important to us.

Eclipses

Generally speaking, an eclipse covers up and prevents light being shed on a situation. Astrologically speaking, this will depend on where the Sun or Moon is positioned in relation to other planets at the time of an eclipse. So if a solar eclipse is in Gemini, there will be a Geminian influence or an influence on Geminis.

Hiding, or shedding, light on an area of our lives is an invitation to pay attention to it. Eclipses are generally about beginnings or endings, which is why our ancestors saw them as portents, important signs to be taken notice of. As it is possible to know when an eclipse is forthcoming, these are charted astronomically; consequently, their astrological significance can be assessed and acted upon ahead of time.

The 10 planets

For the purpose of astrology (but not for astronomy, because the Sun is really a star) we talk about 10 planets, and each astrological sign has a ruling planet, with Mercury, Venus and Mars each being assigned two. The characteristics of each planet describe those influences that can affect signs, all of which information feeds into the interpretation of a birth chart.

The Moon

This sign is an opposing principle to the Sun, forming a pair, and it represents the feminine, symbolising containment and receptivity, how we react most instinctively and with feeling.

Rules the sign of Cancer.

The Sun

The Sun represents the masculine, and is seen as the energy that sparks life, which suggests a paternal energy in our birth chart. It also symbolises our self or essential being, and our purpose.

Rules the sign of Leo.

Mercury

Mercury is the planet of communication and symbolises our urge to make sense of, understand and communicate our thoughts through words.

Rules the signs of Gemini and Virgo.

Venus

The planet of love is all about attraction, connection and pleasure and in a female chart it symbolises her style of femininity, while in a male chart it represents his ideal partner.

Rules the signs of Taurus and Libra.

Mars

This planet symbolises pure energy (Mars was, after all, the god of War) but it also tells you in which areas you're most likely to be assertive, aggressive or to take risks.

Rules the signs of Aries and Scorpio.

Saturn

Saturn is sometimes called the wise teacher or taskmaster of astrology, symbolising lessons learnt and limitations, showing us the value of determination, tenacity and resilience.

Rules the sign of Capricorn.

Jupiter

The planet Jupiter is the largest in our solar system and symbolises bounty and benevolence, all that is expansive and jovial. Like the sign it rules, it's also about moving away from the home on journeys and exploration.

Rules the sign of Sagittarius.

Uranus

This planet symbolises the unexpected, new ideas and innovation, and the urge to tear down the old and usher in the new. The downside can mark an inability to fit in and consequently the feeling of being an outsider.

Rules the sign of Aquarius.

Pluto

Aligned to Hades (*Pluto* in Latin), the god of the underworld or death, this planet exerts a powerful force that lies below the surface and which, in its most negative form, can represent obsessions and compulsive behaviour.

Rules the sign of Scorpio.

Neptune

Linked to the sea, this is about what lies beneath, underwater and too deep to be seen clearly. Sensitive, intuitive and artistic, it also symbolises the capacity to love unconditionally, to forgive and forget.

Rules the sign of Pisces.

The four elements

Further divisions of the 12 astrological signs into the four elements of earth, fire, air and water yield other characteristics. This comes from ancient Greek medicine, where the body was considered to be made up of four bodily fluids or 'humours'. These four humours – blood, yellow bile, black bile and phlegm – corresponded to the four temperaments of sanguine, choleric, melancholic and phlegmatic, to the four seasons of the year, spring, summer, autumn, winter, and the four elements of air, fire, earth and water.

Related to astrology, these symbolic qualities cast further light on characteristics of the different signs. Carl Jung also used them in his psychology, and we still refer to people as earthy, fiery, airy or wet in their approach to life, while sometimes describing people as 'being in their element'. In astrology, those Sun signs that share the same element are said to have an affinity, or an understanding, with each other.

Like all aspects of astrology, there is always a positive and a negative, and a knowledge of any 'shadow side' can be helpful in terms of self-knowledge and what we may need to enhance or balance out, particularly in our dealings with others.

Air

GEMINI ✳ LIBRA ✳ AQUARIUS

The realm of ideas is
where these air signs excel.
Perceptive and visionary and
able to see the big picture,
there is a very reflective
quality to air signs that helps
to vent situations. Too much
air, however, can dissipate
intentions, so Gemini might
be indecisive, Libra has a
tendency to sit on the fence,
while Aquarius can be
very disengaged.

Fire

ARIES ✳ LEO ✳ SAGITTARIUS

There is a warmth and energy
to these signs, a positive
approach, spontaneity
and enthusiasm that can
be inspiring and very
motivational to others.
The downside is that Aries
has a tendency to rush in
headfirst, Leo can have a need
for attention and Sagittarius
can tend to talk it up but
not deliver.

Earth

TAURUS ✳ VIRGO ✳ CAPRICORN

Characteristically, these signs enjoy sensual pleasure, relishing food and other physical satisfactions, and they like to feel grounded, preferring to base their ideas in facts. The downside is that Taureans can be stubborn, Virgos can be pernickety and Capricorns can veer towards a dogged conservatism.

Water

CANCER ✳ SCORPIO ✳ PISCES

Water signs are very responsive, like the tide ebbing and flowing, and can be very perceptive and intuitive, sometimes uncannily so because of their ability to feel. The downside is – watery enough – a tendency to feel swamped, and then Cancer can be both tenacious and self-protective, Pisces chameleon-like in their attention and Scorpio unpredictable and intense.

Cardinal, fixed and mutable signs

In addition to the 12 signs being divided into four elements, they can also be grouped into three different ways in which their energies may act or react, giving further depth to each sign's particular characteristics.

Cardinal

ARIES ✳ CANCER ✳ LIBRA ✳ CAPRICORN

These are action planets, with an energy that takes the initiative and gets things started. Aries has the vision, Cancer the feelings, Libra the contacts and Capricorn the strategy.

Fixed

TAURUS ✳ LEO ✳ SCORPIO ✳ AQUARIUS

Slower but more determined, these signs work to progress and maintain those initiatives that the cardinal signs have fired up. Taurus offers physical comfort, Leo loyalty, Scorpio emotional support and Aquarius sound advice. You can count on fixed signs, but they tend to resist change.

Mutable

GEMINI ✳ VIRGO ✳ SAGITTARIUS ✳ PISCES

Adaptable and responsive to new ideas, places and people, mutable signs have a unique ability to adjust to their surroundings. Gemini is mentally agile, Virgo is practical and versatile, Sagittarius visualises possibilities and Pisces is responsive to change.

The 12 houses

The birth chart is divided into 12 houses, which represent separate areas and functions of your life. When you are told you have something in a specific house – for example, Libra (balance) in the fifth house (creativity and sex) – it creates a way of interpreting the influences that can arise and are particular to how you might approach an aspect of your life.

Each house relates to a Sun sign, and in this way each is represented by some of the characteristics of that sign, which is said to be its natural ruler.

Three of these houses are considered to be mystical, relating to our interior, psychic world: the fourth (home), eighth (death and regeneration) and twelfth (secrets).

1st House

THE SELF

RULED BY ARIES

This house symbolises the self: you, who you are and how you represent yourself, your likes, dislikes and approach to life. It also represents how you see yourself and what you want in life.

2nd House

POSSESSIONS

RULED BY TAURUS

The second house symbolises your possessions, what you own, including money; how you earn or acquire your income; and your material security and the physical things you take with you as you move through life.

3rd House

COMMUNICATION

RULED BY GEMINI

This house is about communication and mental attitude, primarily how you express yourself. It's also about how you function within your family, and how you travel to school or work, and includes how you think, speak, write and learn.

4th House

HOME

RULED BY CANCER

This house is about your roots and your home or homes, present, past and future, so it includes both your childhood and current domestic set-up. It's also about what home and security represents to you.

5th House

CREATIVITY

RULED BY LEO

Billed as the house of creativity and play, this also includes sex, and relates to the creative urge, the libido, in all its manifestations. It's also about speculation in finance and love, games, fun and affection: affairs of the heart.

6th House

HEALTH

RULED BY VIRGO

This house is related to health: our own physical and emotional health, and how robust it is; but also those we care for, look after or provide support to – from family members to work colleagues.

7th House

PARTNERSHIPS

RULED BY LIBRA

The opposite of the first house, this reflects shared goals and intimate partnerships, our choice of life partner and how successful our relationships might be. It also reflects partnerships and adversaries in our professional world.

8th House

REGENERATION

RULED BY SCORPIO

For death, read regeneration or spiritual transformation: this house also reflects legacies and what you inherit after death, in personality traits or materially. And because regeneration requires sex, it's also about sex and sexual emotions.

9th House

TRAVEL

RULED BY SAGITTARIUS

The house of long-distance travel and exploration, this is also about the broadening of the mind that travel can bring, and how that might express itself. It also reflects the sending out of ideas, which can come about from literary effort or publication.

11th House

FRIENDSHIPS

RULED BY AQUARIUS

The eleventh house is about friendship groups and acquaintances, vision and ideas, and is less about immediate gratification but more concerning longer-term dreams and how these might be realised through our ability to work harmoniously with others.

12th House

SECRETS

RULED BY PISCES

Considered the most spiritual house, it is also the house of the unconscious, of secrets and of what might lie hidden, the metaphorical skeleton in the closet. It also reflects the secret ways we might self-sabotage or imprison our own efforts by not exploring them.

10th House

ASPIRATIONS

RULED BY CAPRICORN

This represents our aspiration and status, how we'd like to be elevated in public standing (or not), our ambitions, image and what we'd like to attain in life, through our own efforts.

The ascendant

Otherwise known as your rising sign, this is the sign of the zodiac that appears at the horizon as dawn breaks on the day of your birth, depending on your location in the world and time of birth. This is why knowing your time of birth is a useful factor in astrology, because your 'rising sign' yields a lot of information about those aspects of your character that are more on show, how you present yourself and how you are seen by others. So, even if you are a Sun Capricorn, but have Cancer rising, you may be seen as someone who is maternal, with a noticeable commitment to the domestic life in one way or another. Knowing your own ascendant – or that of another person – will often help explain why there doesn't seem to be such a direct correlation between their personality and their Sun sign.

As long as you know your time of birth and where you were born, working out your ascendant using an online tool or app is very easy (see page 108). Just ask your mum or other family members, or check your birth certificate (in those countries that include a birth time). If the astrological chart were a clock face, the ascendant would be at the 9 o'clock position.

The descendant

The descendant gives an indication of a possible life partner, based on the idea that opposites attract. Once you know your ascendant, the descendant is easy to work out as it is always six signs away: for example, if your ascendant is Virgo, your descendant is Pisces. If the astrological chart were a clock face, the descendant would be at the 3 o'clock position.

The midheaven (MC)

Also included in the birth chart is the position of the midheaven or MC (from the Latin, *medium coeli*, meaning middle of the heavens), which indicates your attitude towards your work, career and professional standing. If the astrological chart were a clock face, the MC would be at the 12 o'clock position.

The IC

Finally, your IC (from the Latin, *imum coeli*, meaning the lowest part of the heavens) indicates your attitude towards your home and family, and is also related to the end of your life. Your IC will be directly opposite your MC: for example, if your MC is Aquarius, your IC is Leo. If the astrological chart were a clock face, the IC would be at the 6 o'clock position.

Saturn return

Saturn is one of the slower-moving planets, taking around 28 years to complete its orbit around the Sun and return to the place it occupied at the time of your birth. This return can last between two to three years and be very noticeable in the period coming up to our thirtieth and sixtieth birthdays, often considered to be significant 'milestone' birthdays.

Because the energy of Saturn is sometimes experienced as demanding, this isn't always an easy period of life. A wise teacher or a hard taskmaster, some consider the Saturn effect as 'cruel to be kind' in the way that many good teachers can be, keeping us on track like a rigorous personal trainer.

Everyone experiences their Saturn return relevant to their circumstances, but it is a good time to take stock, let go of the stuff in your life that no longer serves you and revise your expectations, while being unapologetic about what you would like to include more of in your life. So if you are experiencing or anticipating this life event, embrace and work with it because what you learn now – about yourself, mainly – is worth knowing, however turbulent it might be, and can pay dividends in how you manage the next 28 years!

Mercury retrograde

Even those with little interest in astrology often take notice when the planet Mercury is retrograde. Astrologically, retrogrades are periods when planets are stationary but, as we continue to move forwards, Mercury 'appears' to move backwards. There is a shadow period either side of a retrograde period, when it could be said to be slowing down or speeding up, which can also be a little turbulent. Generally speaking, the advice is not to make any important moves related to communication on a retrograde and, even if a decision is made, know that it's likely to change.

Given that Mercury is the planet of communication, you can immediately see why there are concerns about its retrograde status and its link to communication failures – of the old-fashioned sort when the post office loses a letter, or the more modern technological variety when your computer crashes

– causing problems. Mercury retrograde can also affect travel, with delays in flights or train times, traffic jams or collisions. Mercury also influences personal communications: listening, speaking, being heard (or not), and can cause confusion or arguments. It can also affect more formal agreements, like contracts between buyer and seller.

These retrograde periods occur three to four times a year, lasting for roughly three weeks, with a shadow period either side. The dates in which it happens also mean it occurs within a specific astrological sign. If, for example, it occurs between 25 October and 15 November, its effect would be linked to the characteristics of Scorpio. In addition, those Sun sign Scorpios, or those with Scorpio in significant placements in their chart, may also experience a greater effect.

Mercury retrograde dates are easy to find from an astrological table, or ephemeris, and online. These can be used in order to avoid planning events that might be affected around these times. How Mercury retrograde may affect you more personally requires knowledge of your birth chart and an understanding of its more specific combination of influences with the signs and planets in your chart.

If you are going to weather a Mercury retrograde more easily, be aware that glitches can occur so, to some extent, expect delays and double-check details. Stay positive if postponements occur and consider this period an opportunity to slow down, review or reconsider ideas in your business or your personal life. Use the time to correct mistakes or reshape plans, preparing for when any stuck energy can shift and you can move forward again more smoothly.

Further reading

Astrology Decoded (2013) by Sue Merlyn Farebrother; published by Rider

Astrology for Dummies (2007) by Rae Orion; published by Wiley Publishing

Chart Interpretation Handbook: Guidelines for Understanding the Essentials of the Birth Chart (1990) by Stephen Arroyo; published by CRCS Publications

Jung's Studies in Astrology (2018) by Liz Greene; published by RKP

The Only Astrology Book You'll Ever Need (2012) by Joanne Woolfolk; published by Taylor Trade

Websites

astro.com

astrologyzone.com

jessicaadams.com

shelleyvonstrunkel.com

Apps

Astrostyle

Co-Star

Susan Miller's Astrology Zone

The Daily Horoscope

The Pattern

Time Passages

Acknowledgements

Particular thanks are due to my trusty
team of Taureans. Firstly, to Kate Pollard,
Publishing Director at Hardie Grant, for her
passion for beautiful books and for commissioning
this series. And to Bex Fitzsimons for all her good
natured and conscientious editing. And finally to
Evi O. Studio, whose illustration and design talents
have produced small works of art. With such a
star-studded team, these books can only
shine and for that, my thanks.

About the author

Stella Andromeda has been studying
astrology for over 30 years, believing that
a knowledge of the constellations of the
skies and their potential for psychological
interpretation can be a useful tool. This
extension of her study into book form makes
modern insights about the ancient wisdom
of the stars easily accessible, sharing her
passion that reflection and self-knowledge
only empowers us in life. With her sun in
Taurus, Aquarius ascendant and Moon
in Cancer, she utilises earth, air and water
to inspire her own astrological journey.

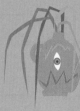

Published in 2019 by Hardie Grant Books,
an imprint of Hardie Grant Publishing

Hardie Grant Books (London)
5th & 6th Floors
52–54 Southwark Street
London, SE1 1UN

Hardie Grant Books (Melbourne)
Building 1, 658 Church Street
Richmond, Victoria 3121

hardiegrantbooks.com

British Library Cataloguing-in-Publication Data. A catalogue record
for this book is available from the British Library.

Capricorn
ISBN: 9781784882679

10 9 8 7 6 5 4

Publishing Director: Kate Pollard
Junior Editor: Bex Fitzsimons
Art Direction and Illustrations: Evi O. Studio
Editor: Wendy Hobson
Production Controller: Sinead Hering

Colour reproduction by p2d
Printed and bound in China by Leo Paper Products Ltd.